# Eek, Amphibians!



Candice Ransom

Lerner Publications ◆ Minneapolis

Lerner Publications Company
An imprint of Lerner Publishing Group, Inc.
241 First Avenue North
Minneapolis, MN 55401 USA

For reading levels and more information, look up this title at www.lernerbooks.com.

Main body text set in Billy Infant Regular. Typeface provided by SparkyType.

**Editor:** Nicole Berglund **Designer:** Martha Kranes **Photo Editor:** Nicole Berglund

**Library of Congress Cataloging-in-Publication Data**

Names: Ransom, Candice F., 1952- author.
Title: Eek, amphibians! / Candice Ransom.
Description: Minneapolis : Lerner Publications, [2026] | Series: Lightning bolt books. Creepy creatures | Includes bibliographical references and index. | Audience: Ages 6-9 | Audience: Grades 2-3 | Summary: "Frogs hop and salamanders slink. Readers discover some of the world's spookiest amphibians, from the deadly rough-skinned newt to the Congolese giant toad that shares the markings of a fierce snake"— Provided by publisher.
Identifiers: LCCN 2024038760 (print) | LCCN 2024038761 (ebook) | ISBN 9798765668986 (lib. bdg.) | ISBN 9798765684597 (pbk.) | ISBN 9798765679654 (epub)
Subjects: LCSH: Amphibians—Juvenile literature.
Classification: LCC QL644.2 .R36 2026 (print) | LCC QL644.2 (ebook) | DDC 597.8—dc23/eng/20240911

LC record available at https://lccn.loc.gov/2024038760
LC ebook record available at https://lccn.loc.gov/2024038761

Manufactured in the United States of America
1-1011577-53869-9/26/2024

# Table of Contents

# Killer Newt

A small brown newt walks along a creek. A hungry heron steps in front of the newt. The surprised newt raises its head and bends its tail over its back.

**It shows its bright orange belly as a warning.** But the heron swallows the newt. Minutes later, the bird is dead. Unharmed, the newt crawls out of the heron's mouth.

A rough-skinned newt gives a warning.

The rough-skinned newt is an amphibian. Amphibians are such animals as frogs, toads, salamanders, and newts. Most begin life in water as eggs. Then they live on land.

The rough-skinned newt may be the most poisonous animal on Earth. **But most amphibians are not dangerous.**

A Javan tree frog

# Small but Creepy

The Congolese giant toad is only 5.5 inches (14 cm) long. It lives in African rainforests.

The toad has the same markings as the head of the Gaboon viper. Animals are afraid of the viper so they avoid the toad. **The harmless amphibian has a perfect disguise!**

Gaboon vipers have venom that harms the animals they bite.

The turtle frog does not look like most frogs. It looks like a pink blob. It has small eyes, a small head, and short legs.

Turtle frogs live in burrows about 3 feet (1 m) below the ground.

Turtle frogs live in Australia's desert. To keep cool, they burrow in the sand during the day. At night, they come out to eat termites.

Female turtle frogs do not lay eggs in water as most frogs do. They lay up to fifty eggs in their sandy burrows. When the eggs hatch, tiny pink frogs hop out.

A burrow in sand

Olm salamanders live in caves in Europe. These aquatic creatures live in total darkness.

An olm swims in a cave.

Their bodies are ghostly white. They breathe through gills. Olms are blind but can hear when food such as bugs or snails are nearby.

Olms have eyes hidden beneath their skin that allow them to see light.

The olm can live to be more than one hundred years old!

Food is hard to find in caves. Olms don't move much to save energy until their next meal. Scientists believe these salamanders can live ten years without eating!

# Slimy and Icky

A frog leaps into a pond. A salamander darts under a leaf. A toad hops in a garden. Many people are startled by their sudden movements.

Amphibians are small creatures. Most people don't notice amphibians. They are most active at night.

Some people think amphibians are icky. Others think their damp skin feels slimy. Most amphibians are harmless to humans.

A spring salamander

Amphibians eat insects that destroy crops. They are also food for other animals. **They are an important part of the world.**

# Spooky or Cute?

The tiny glass frog is green on top. But underneath, its skin is see-through. Its heart, liver, and stomach can be seen. Other animals often don't see glass frogs. Is this frog spooky or cute? What do you think?

# Amphibian Facts

- One rough-skinned newt has enough poison to kill twenty-five thousand mice!
- The Chinese giant salamander is about 6 feet (1.8 m) long. It is the largest amphibian in the world.
- The female Surinam toad hatches her eggs on her back. The babies come out as tiny toads.

## Glossary

**amphibian:** a type of animal that includes frogs, toads, salamanders, and newts. Amphibians are born in the water and can live in water and on land.

**aquatic:** an animal that lives in water

**desert:** dry areas that have a lack of water

**gill:** a body part that allows young amphibians to breathe underwater

**poisonous:** containing poison

**startled:** surprised or frightened

**termite:** an insect that eats wood

**viper:** any snake that has venom in its bite

## Learn More

Britannica Kids: Amphibian
https://kids.britannica.com/kids/article/amphibian/352745

Brody, Walt. *Chinese Giant Salamanders: Nature's Biggest Amphibian*. Minneapolis: Lerner Publications, 2024.

Hughes, Sloane. *20 Things You Didn't Know about Amphibian Adaptations*. New York: PowerKids, 2023.

Humphrey, Natalie. *It's an Amphibian!* Buffalo: Gareth Stevens, 2025.

*National Geographic Kids*: Amphibians
https://kids.nationalgeographic.com/animals/amphibians

*Time for Kids*: Amphibian Facts
https://www.timeforkids.com/k1/amphibian-facts-k1/

# Index



## Photo Acknowledgments


Image credits: Wirestock/Getty Images, pp. 4, 6; ZUMA Press, Inc./Alamy, p. 5; kuritafsheen/Getty Images, p. 7; Tom McHugh/Science Source, p. 8; Daniel Hernanz Ramos/Getty Images, p. 9; Wikimedia Commons (CC 2.5), p. 10; Mohd Sazli Ab Hamid/Getty Images, p. 11; Danielli.capture/Shutterstock, p. 12; gremlin/Getty Images, p. 13; Nature Picture Library/Alamy, p. 14; blickwinkel/Alamy, p. 15; Robert Pickett/Getty Images, p. 16; Jason Edwards/Getty Images, p. 17; Ethan Ramirez/Getty Images, p. 18; Cathy Keifer/Shutterstock, p. 19; Lukas Gogh/Shutterstock, p. 20.

Cover: Wikimedia Commons (CC 4.0).